I AM NOT A TOILET PAPER ROLL

THE RECYCLING PROJECT BOOK

10 INCREDIBLE THINGS TO MAKE WITH TOILET PAPER ROLLS!

First edition for North America published in 2018
by Barron's Educational Series, Inc.

Text and design copyright © 2018 Carlton Books Limited

Published in 2018 by Carlton Books Limited, an imprint of the
Carlton Publishing Group, 20 Mortimer Street, London W1T 3JW

All inquiries should be addressed to:
Barron's Educational Series, Inc.
250 Wireless Boulevard
Hauppauge, NY 11788
www.barronseduc.com

ISBN: 978-1-4380-1244-5

Library of Congress Control Number: 2018941668

Date of Manufacture: July 2018
Manufactured by: RRD Asia, Kowloon, Hong Kong

Printed in China
9 8 7 6 5 4 3 2 1

Creative Director: Clare Baggaley
Written, designed, illustrated, and packaged by: Dynamo Limited

I AM NOT A TOILET PAPER ROLL

THE RECYCLING PROJECT BOOK

BARRON'S

10 INCREDIBLE THINGS TO MAKE WITH TOILET PAPER ROLLS!

Hi THERE!

ARE YOU READY TO GET STARTED? OF COURSE YOU ARE!

THIS CRAFT BOOK IS JAM-PACKED WITH RECYCLABLE ARTY PROJECTS AND SIMPLE STEP-BY-STEP GUIDES. YOU'LL FIND OUT HOW TO TURN EMPTY TOILET PAPER ROLLS INTO UNICORNS, SHARKS, PIRATES, AND SO MUCH MORE!

IF YOU'D LIKE, YOU CAN USE OUR HANDY CUTOUT PIECES AT THE BACK OF YOUR BOOK TO HELP YOU WITH YOUR CRAFTS.

YOU WILL NEED

- LOTS OF EMPTY TOILET PAPER ROLLS
- TAPE
- GLUE
- COLORFUL PAPER
- COLORFUL CARDSTOCK
- FINGER PAINTS
- PAINTBRUSHES
- SAFETY SCISSORS
- STRING
- TIN FOIL
- GLITTER
- LOLLIPOP STICKS
- PENS
- PENCILS

YOU'LL NEED A GROWN-UP TO HELP YOU WITH ALL OF THE PROJECTS!

CONTENTS

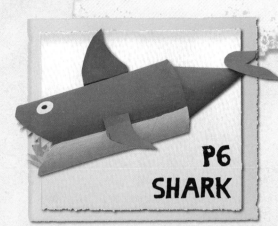

SHAAAAARK!

I'M A **TERRIFYING** SHARK HERE TO **CHOMP** ON UNSUSPECTING **TOES** IN THE **BATHTUB!** I DEFINITELY WOULDN'T TURN TO TOILET PAPER ROLL MUSH UNDERWATER.

YOU WILL NEED

- ONE EMPTY TOILET PAPER ROLL
- BLUE AND WHITE PAINT
- PAINTBRUSH & PEN
- SAFETY SCISSORS
- BLUE & WHITE CARDSTOCK
- A BOWL (TO DRAW AROUND)
- TAPE
- GOOGLY EYES

WATCH OUT!!

SET THE SCENE

Make your shark a perfect undersea background by tearing up strips of blue tissue paper and sticking them onto some cardboard. Add pieces of tin foil to make the water really sparkle! Use finger paints to make orange and pink coral on the seafloor. Are you ready to make this toothy toilet paper roll into a dangerous shark? Turn the page to find out how!

DID YOU KNOW? BABY SHARKS ARE CALLED PUPS!

GO FURTHER!

NEXT, USE THESE SKILLS TO MAKE A CHOMPY ALLIGATOR. TURN THE PAGE TO FIND OUT HOW!

I'M A SHARK!

1

Paint your toilet paper roll so that one half is white and the other half is blue. When the paint is completely dry, cut two triangles out of the end of the toilet paper roll to make the shark's mouth.

2

To make the tail, draw a circle on the blue cardstock by tracing around a bowl (a cereal bowl would be perfect). Then carefully cut a large triangle out of the circle, just like the picture above.

3

Roll the two sides of your blue circle together to make a cone and tape it in place. Slot the cone into the end of the toilet paper roll and tape them together.

4

Add extra details by cutting these tail and fin shapes from your blue cardstock, then tape them on. You can also add a shape for the shark's eyes.

5

Create a set of pointy teeth by cutting zigzags out of two strips of white cardstock. Glue them along the top and bottom of the shark's mouth.

6

Complete your fearsome shark by adding some googly eyes from the back of your book.

I AM NOT A TOILET PAPER ROLL...
I'M AN ALLIGATOR!

This time, paint 2 toilet paper rolls green and tape them together to make the body. Snip in a mouth shape, just like last time, and add your spiky teeth. Then, cut a pointy tail and feet from green cardstock and stick on googly eyes. Finally, cut out triangles from green cardstock and glue these to the alligator's back!

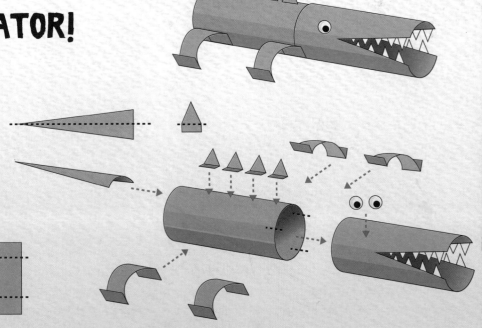

BAT!

I'M A BRILLIANT BLACK BAT, CAN'T YOU SEE?

I SLEEP DANGLING UPSIDE DOWN FROM THE VERY TALLEST OF TREES.

I ONLY COME OUT AFTER DARK WHEN I FLAP MY BIG WINGS AND SOAR THROUGH THE STARS.

YOU WILL NEED
- ONE EMPTY TOILET PAPER ROLL
- BLACK PAINT AND A BRUSH
- TAPE & GLUE
- BLACK AND WHITE CARDSTOCK
- SAFETY SCISSORS
- GOOGLY EYES

SET THE SCENE

Create a background for your bat using night-time colors—dark blue or black work best! Paint a shiny moon and stars in yellow, or cut them out using tin foil and tape or glue them down. Add a sprinkle of glitter for shooting stars, too. Turn the page to find out how to make your very own bat-tastic buddy in six easy steps!

IT'S SO COMFY SNOOZING UPSIDE DOWN. ZZZZ!

DID YOU KNOW?
THERE ARE OVER 1,000 DIFFERENT TYPES OF BAT SPECIES ON THE PLANET!

GO FURTHER!

IN ADDITION TO A BAT, YOU CAN ALSO MAKE A FOX OR PEACOCK USING THIS TECHNIQUE. JUST TURN THE PAGE AND WE WILL SHOW YOU HOW.

I'M A BAT!

1

Fold the top ends of your toilet paper roll toward each other to give your bat some ears. Now do the same to the bottom of your toilet paper roll to make the bat's feet. Tape the shape in place if needed.

2

Paint your toilet paper roll in your battiest black all over, then leave to dry while you do Step 3.

3

To make your bat's wings, carefully cut a big "m" shape out of black cardstock. Snip some points along the bottom edge, like the picture above.

4

When your painted toilet paper roll is dry, use a dab of glue to stick it to the middle of your wings.

5

Take a pair of googly eyes and place them toward the top of your toilet paper roll, under the ears.

6

Finally, give your bat some spooky fangs by cutting two small triangles out of white cardstock. Glue them on and your bat is ready to take flight!

I AM NOT A TOILET PAPER ROLL...
I'M A FOX!

To make your fox, paint a toilet paper roll orange and only fold over the top of the toilet paper roll, not the bottom. Then, replace the bat wings with a bushy tail shape cut out from orange and white cardstock and tape it to the back of the fox's body. For the face, cut out a white heart shape and add googly eyes and black whiskers.

I AM NOT A TOILET PAPER ROLL...
I'M A PEACOCK!

If you can make a fox, then you can make a peacock! Look at the diagram and you will see that the same teardrop shape that is used for the fox tail can be used for a peacock's feathers. Also, use the heart shape, but on it's tummy this time! And add the peacock's cute feet!

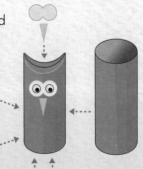

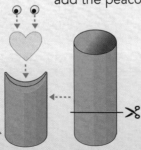

13

ELEPHANT!

WITH MY HUGE FEET AND A "TOOT" OF MY TRUNK, I MAKE QUITE A RACKET. NO TOILET PAPER ROLL COULD EVER BE AS NOISY AS ME!

STOMP, STOMP, STOMP!

YOU WILL NEED	
	● ONE EMPTY TOILET PAPER ROLL
	● WHITE, BLACK, AND GRAY PAINT
	● PAINTBRUSH
	● BLACK PEN OR PENCIL
	● GLUE
	● GOOGLY EYES

SET THE SCENE

Make a jungle scene for your elephant pal by layering different shades of green. You could even try making tree trunks from kitchen roll tubes painted brown. Turn the page to see how to make a rumble in the jungle by turning your toilet paper roll into a mighty elephant.

Turn the page to see how to make a rumble in the jungle by turning your toilet paper roll into a mighty elephant.

DID YOU KNOW? ELEPHANTS ARE THE LARGEST LAND MAMMAL AND THEY LIVE TOGETHER IN GROUPS LED BY THE OLDEST FEMALE.

TRUMPETY! TRUMPETY!

GO FURTHER!

YOU CAN MAKE AN EIGHT-LEGGED OCTOPUS PAL FROM A TOILET PAPER ROLL, TOO! WE'LL SHOW YOU EXACTLY WHAT TO DO ON THE NEXT PAGES.

I'M AN ELEPHANT!

1

For the trunk, make two cuts from the bottom of the toilet paper roll until you reach about halfway up.

2

Carefully cut big ear shapes on each side of your toilet paper roll (be sure to leave enough room for the elephant's face in the middle). Then, fold the ears forward to make them stick out.

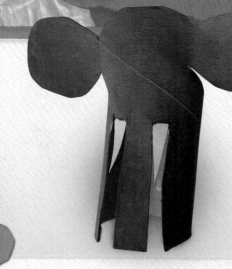

3

Cut two long, thin triangles on either side of the first cuts you made, leaving two tusk shapes at the top of each one. Now paint your elephant!

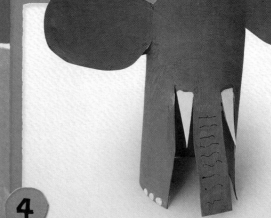

4

When the paint is dry, dot toenails onto the elephant's feet using the other end of the paintbrush. Add more details with black pen.

5

Stick on some googly eyes from the back of your book to make your elephant come to life!

6

Paint a shadow onto the ears of your elephant using black paint to add a bit of extra detail.

I AM NOT A TOILET PAPER ROLL...
I'M AN OCTOPUS!

Do you fancy making an octopus instead? Carefully snip the base of your toilet paper roll into eight legs—you should aim to cut about halfway up the toilet paper roll. Then fold down the legs, like this. Finally, paint your octopus in bright colors and let it dry before adding some googly eyes.

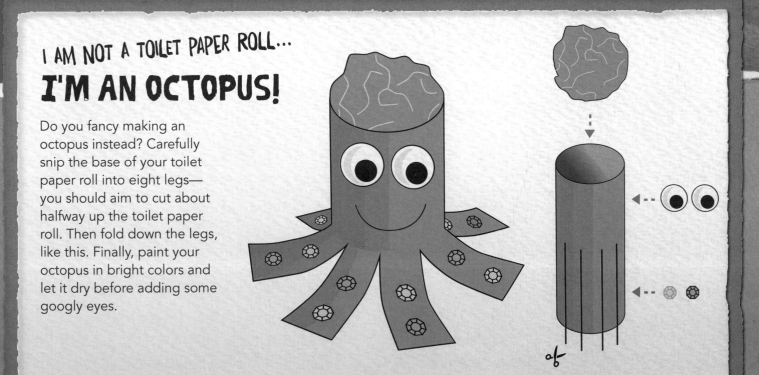

ROCKET!

ZOOM! UP, UP, AND AWAY I GO! I AM A ROCKET—DON'T YOU KNOW? JUST LOOK AT ME GO AS I SOAR THROUGH SPACE. THERE'S NO WAY THAT I HAVE BEEN MADE FROM TISSUE PAPER AND PAINTS!

YOU WILL NEED

- ONE TOILET PAPER ROLL
- COLORED PAINT
- COLORED CARDSTOCK
- SAFETY SCISSORS
- TAPE & GLUE
- TIN FOIL
- TISSUE PAPER

SET THE SCENE

Decorate a piece of black cardstock with tin foil, silver stars, and colorful planets for an out-of-this-world background. Paint the planets, copy them from a book, or cut pictures out of a magazine. Want to make your very own awesome rocket? Of course you do! Blast off to the next page to find out how…

DID YOU KNOW?
HUMANS FIRST LANDED (AND WALKED!) ON THE MOON IN 1969.

I'M OFF TO VISIT THE MOON...

GO FURTHER!

IF YOU DON'T LIKE MAKING ROCKETS, YOU CAN TRY THESE FANTASTIC FAIRY HOUSES INSTEAD. TURN THE PAGE AND WE'LL SHOW YOU JUST WHAT TO DO.

I'M A ROCKET!

1

Paint your toilet paper roll all over in any color you like (we've gone for rocket red!). Leave to dry.

2

Make a circle by drawing around a large roll of tape or a cereal bowl and cut it out. Snip out a large triangle, like above, and roll it into a cone shape. Use some tape to keep it in place.

3

Tape the cone in place on top of the rocket, and then stick on some tin foil circles to make portholes.

4

Tear fire-colored (red, orange, and yellow) tissue paper into strips.

Tape the shredded tissue paper to the inside of the rocket at the bottom.

5

Now that you know how, you can make lots of different colorful rockets! Get creative by decorating them in fun ways.

6

I AM NOT A TOILET PAPER ROLL...
I'M A FAIRY HOUSE!

Making fairy houses from toilet paper rolls is almost the same as making rockets. This time, when you make your paper cone, cut to give it a zigzag edge. Next snip in a little door for your fairies to come and go as they please, and make windows from paper or paint them on—it's up to you!

PIRATE!

AHOY THERE, MATEY! I BE A PIRATE AND I'VE SAILED THE **SEVEN SEAS** ON MY SHIP IN SEARCH OF **TREASURE.** ANYONE WHO SAYS I'M A TOILET PAPER ROLL CAN **WALK THE PLANK!**

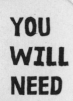

YOU WILL NEED

- ONE EMPTY TOILET PAPER ROLL
- PAINTS & PAINTBRUSHES
- WHITE PAPER
- SAFETY SCISSORS
- GLUE
- BLACK CARDSTOCK
- BLACK PEN
- BLUE OAKTAG
- OPTIONAL: TISSUE PAPER

SET THE SCENE

Make an island scene for your pirate ship with a sheet of blue oaktag for the sea and a yellow paper desert island stuck on top. Now you're ready for treasure hunting. "X" marks the spot! Ready to make your pirate pal? Turn the page to find out how.

AARRRGH, M'HEARTIES!

DID YOU KNOW?

LOTS OF PIRATE SHIPS HAVE A FLAG WITH A SKULL AND CROSSBONES ON IT. THIS IS CALLED THE JOLLY ROGER.

GO FURTHER!

MAKE A TOILET PAPER ROLL TREASURE CHEST FOR YOUR PIRATES TO KEEP THEIR PRECIOUS TREASURE IN! TURN THE PAGE TO FOLLOW OUR SIMPLE STEP-BY-STEP GUIDE.

I'M A PIRATE!

1

Paint half of your toilet paper roll in a skin color of your choice and then leave it to dry.

2

To make a striped top, cut a strip of paper (6 in x 2 in [16 cm x 5 cm]). Now paint or draw some stripes.

3

Glue the top on your pirate, and then paint the bottom of the toilet paper roll black for the trousers.

4

Cut a pirate hat shape out of black cardstock. Then cut out a skull and cross from white paper and glue this onto the hat.

5

Tape your hat to the top of your toilet paper roll. Draw your pirate's face with a black pen and add an eye patch for the finishing touch. Aarrrgh! M'hearties! Ready to set sail!

6

If you prefer, you could make a bandana for your pirate buddy! Just wrap tissue paper around your pirate's head and make a little knot shape to one side.

I AM NOT A TOILET PAPER ROLL...
I'M A TREASURE CHEST!

First, cut a toilet paper roll in half widthways to make the curved lid of the chest. Then cut a toilet paper roll in half lengthways and flatten out the cardstock. Then make folds in the flattened out cardstock to tape it into a box shape. Next, pop the lid inside and paint to decorate your chest. Add yellow strips of cardstock to secure the lid.

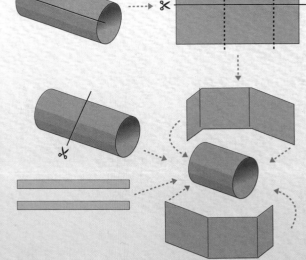

UNICORN!

NO, YOU'RE NOT DREAMING, I AM A **MAGICAL UNICORN** AND I'M HERE TO MAKE FRIENDS WITH YOU! **GRANTING WISHES** AND MAKING YOUR **DREAMS COME TRUE** IS ALL I'VE EVER WANTED TO DO.

YOU WILL NEED

- ONE EMPTY TOILET PAPER ROLL
- WHITE, PINK, & BLACK PAINT
- SAFETY SCISSORS
- COLORFUL TISSUE PAPER
- WHITE AND PINK CARDSTOCK
- GLUE & TAPE
- GLITTER
- RAINBOW TISSUE PAPER
- GOOGLY EYES

JOIN MY UNICORN SQUAD!

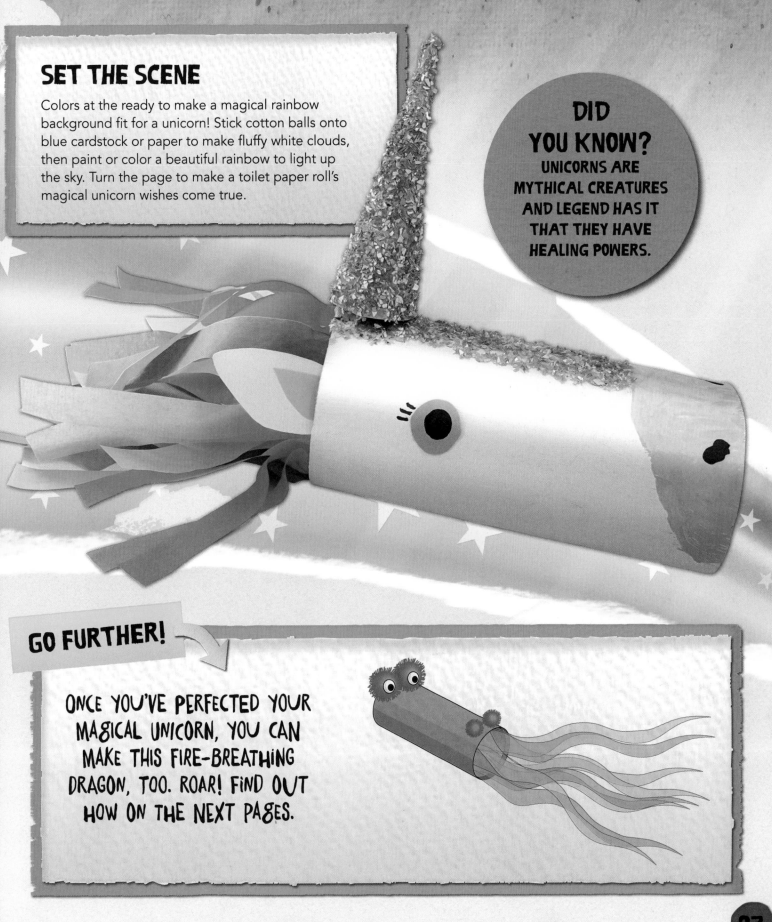

SET THE SCENE

Colors at the ready to make a magical rainbow background fit for a unicorn! Stick cotton balls onto blue cardstock or paper to make fluffy white clouds, then paint or color a beautiful rainbow to light up the sky. Turn the page to make a toilet paper roll's magical unicorn wishes come true.

DID YOU KNOW? UNICORNS ARE MYTHICAL CREATURES AND LEGEND HAS IT THAT THEY HAVE HEALING POWERS.

GO FURTHER!

ONCE YOU'VE PERFECTED YOUR MAGICAL UNICORN, YOU CAN MAKE THIS FIRE-BREATHING DRAGON, TOO. ROAR! FIND OUT HOW ON THE NEXT PAGES.

I AM NOT A TOILET PAPER ROLL...

I'M A UNICORN!

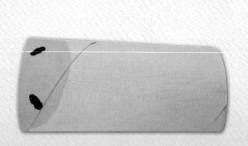

1

Paint your toilet paper roll white with a pink semicircle at the end. When it is dry, dab on two black nostrils using the other end of a paintbrush.

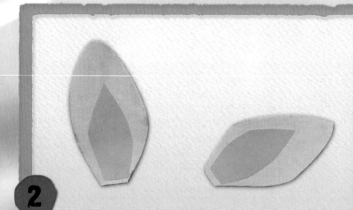

2

Carefully cut out two ear shapes from white cardstock, and then cut out smaller ear shapes in pink to make the insides of the ears. Glue them together.

3

To make the unicorn's horn, cut a triangle out of cardstock, roll it into a cone shape, and tape it in place. Next cover the cone in glue and sprinkle with gold glitter until it is completely covered.

4

Carefully tape the horn onto the top of the unicorn. Then add a thick line of glue from the horn to the nose and sprinkle this with glitter.

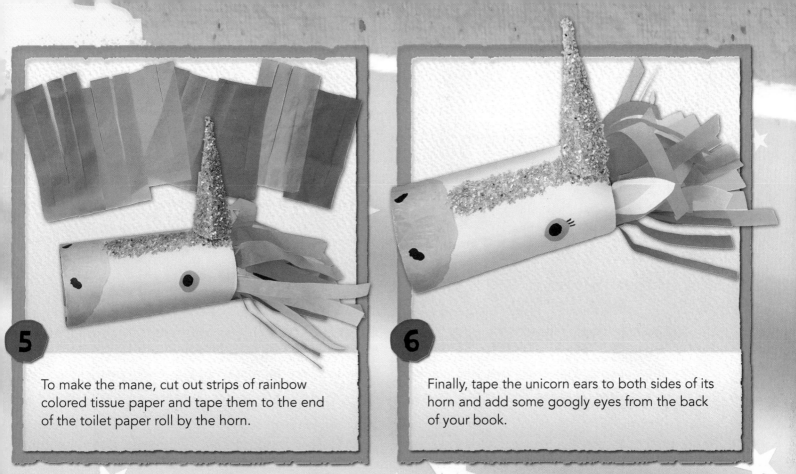

5

To make the mane, cut out strips of rainbow colored tissue paper and tape them to the end of the toilet paper roll by the horn.

6

Finally, tape the unicorn ears to both sides of its horn and add some googly eyes from the back of your book.

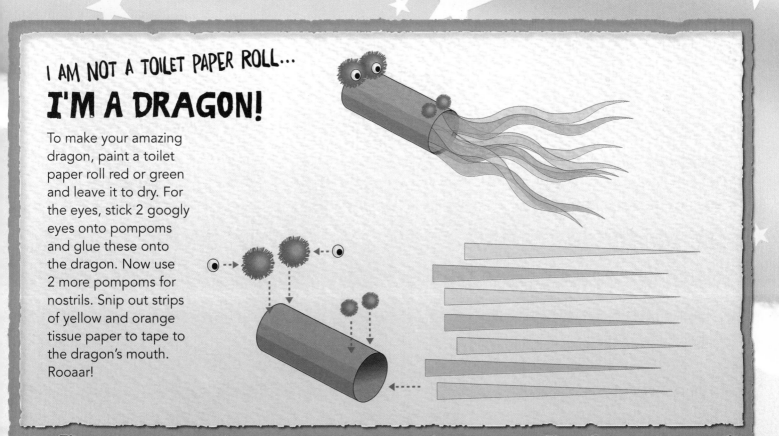

I AM NOT A TOILET PAPER ROLL...
I'M A DRAGON!

To make your amazing dragon, paint a toilet paper roll red or green and leave it to dry. For the eyes, stick 2 googly eyes onto pompoms and glue these onto the dragon. Now use 2 more pompoms for nostrils. Snip out strips of yellow and orange tissue paper to tape to the dragon's mouth. Rooaar!

NINJAAAA!

WATCH ME ROLL WITH MY **AWESOME NINJA SKILLS.** I'M THE SPEEDIEST AND MOST **POWERFUL NINJA AROUND** SO THERE'S **NO WAY** THAT I AM A TOILET PAPER ROLL.

HI-YAH!

YOU WILL NEED

- ONE EMPTY TOILET PAPER ROLL
- DARK PAINT
- SAFETY SCISSORS
- PINK PAPER
- BLACK PEN
- GLUE
- BLACK CARDSTOCK
- STRING

SET THE SCENE

Cut out rectangles from tracing paper and stick them onto a sheet of black cardstock to make a cool Dojo-style background. Want to give a toilet paper roll some nifty ninja moves? You can make your nimble ninja on the next page.

DID YOU KNOW? NINJAS ORIGINALLY CAME FROM JAPAN AND WERE CALLED SHINOBI-NO-MONO.

I'M A MARTIAL ARTS MASTER!

GO FURTHER!

TAKE YOUR PROJECT TO THE NEXT LEVEL BY MAKING A HORSE FOR YOUR NINJA TO RIDE. TURN THE PAGE TO FIND OUT HOW.

I'M A NINJA!

1

Paint a toilet paper roll any color you like (we recommend a dark color) and leave it to dry.

2

Cut a small rectangle from pink paper and draw on some eyes. This will be your ninja's face.

3

Glue the face onto the toilet paper roll, and then carefully cut some small rectangles out of black cardstock and glue them over your ninja's eyes to make eyebrows.

4

Next, cut out another thin rectangle from black card (4 in [10 cm]) and get your length of string ready.

5

Tie the string around the ninja's waist and slide the card stick inside, like this.

6

Now you can make a whole ninja crew using different colors. Sayonara for now!

I AM NOT A TOILET PAPER ROLL...
I'M A HORSE!

Tape two toilet paper rolls together, like this, to make the horse's head and body. Cut out and slide in a circle of card for the horse's nose and give it some nostrils with black paint. Cut out four legs from cardstock and tape these in place so that your horse is ready to gallop. Make pointy paper ears and add two googly eyes. Wool or yarn makes a great mane and tail!

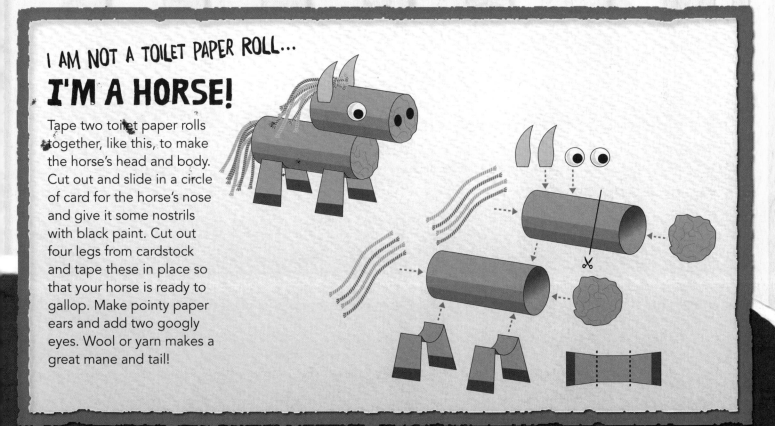

GINGERBREAD MAN!

HELLO THERE! I'M A **FRIENDLY GINGERBREAD MAN**, SWEET AS CAN BE. MY BUTTONS ARE MADE FROM DELICIOUS **CANDY**, NOT PAPER AND GLUE.

YOU WILL NEED

- ONE EMPTY TOILET PAPER ROLL
- ORANGE PAINT & PAINTBRUSH
- SAFETY SCISSORS
- ORANGE CARDSTOCK
- STICKY TAPE
- COLORFUL PAPER
- GLUE

SET THE SCENE

Make a cunning fox out of orange and brown paper to help the gingerbread man get across a river of torn blue paper. But watch out for the fox's tricks! Ready to make your toilet paper roll gingerbread man? Turn the page to find out how.

Turn the page to find out how.

I LOVE MY FANCY BOW TIE!

DID YOU KNOW? THE BIGGEST GINGERBREAD HOUSE EVER WAS 21 FT TALL AND MADE IN TEXAS!

GO FURTHER!

YOU COULD MAKE A SUPER COOL CLOWN USING THIS TECHNIQUE! FIND OUT HOW ON PAGE 37.

FIND OUT HOW ON PAGE 37.

I'M A GINGERBREAD MAN!

1

Paint a toilet paper roll all over with orange or yellow paint and leave it to the side to dry.

2

Next, cut a balloon shape (as above) out of orange cardstock. Use colored paper or marker pens to create your gingerbread man's face.

3

Tape the head to the top of the toilet paper roll.

4

Now, carefully cut two strips of orange cardstock (6 in x 1 in [15 cm x 3 cm]) for the legs, and two strips (6 in x 1 in [15 cm x 2 cm]) for the arms.

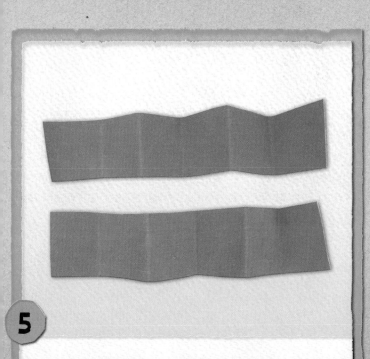

5 Fold the strips of cardstock like this, to make them springy. Then use tape to attach the arms and legs to the body.

6 Decorate your new gingerbread buddy by sticking on colorful paper buttons and a bright bow tie.

7 Make a simple candy cane by cutting out this shape from cardstock and painting on some bright red stripes.

I AM NOT A TOILET PAPER ROLL...
I'M A CLOWN!

Paint your toilet paper roll and then add your colorful bow tie and buttons. This time, you'll need white cardstock for the face! Draw on some black crosses for eyes, and then add a red smiley mouth and round nose. Cut out arms and big feet from cardstock to tape in place and use wool to make hair.

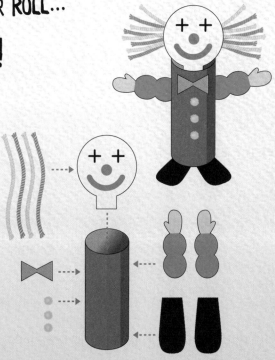

CASTLE!

I'M A **BEAUTIFUL** CASTLE! I'M HOME TO THE **FINEST ROYALTY**. WITH MY TALL TOWERS TOPPED WITH **FABULOUS FLAGS**, I'M FAR TOO **GRAND** TO BE MADE FROM CARDBOARD!

- THREE EMPTY TOILET PAPER ROLLS
- SAFETY SCISSORS
- PAINTS & PAINTBRUSHES
- PAPER
- GLUE
- LOLLIPOP STICKS OR TOOTHPICKS
- BLUE, GREEN, & BROWN PAPER
- PEN
- TAPE

SET THE SCENE

Pop your castle onto layers of green paper to make rolling countryside. Add trees like these shown or scrunch up tissue paper for colorful flowers. Turn the page to find out how to transform three toilet paper rolls into a splendid castle fit for a king and queen.

DID YOU KNOW? MOATS PROTECT CASTLES AND KEEP OUT ANY UNWELCOME VISITORS.

GO FURTHER!

WHY STOP AT JUST THREE CASTLE TOWERS? LET'S MAKE YOUR CASTLE EVEN MORE SPECTACULAR! WE WILL SHOW YOU HOW ON THE NEXT PAGES.

I'M A CASTLE!

1

Cut rectangles from the top of your toilet paper roll to create turrets.

2

Repeat Step 1 on two more toilet paper rolls. You could make some towers shorter by trimming the tops off first.

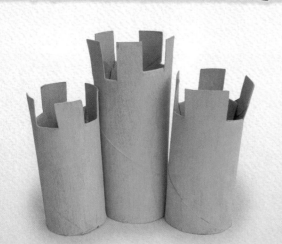

3

Paint all the toilet paper rolls in your favorite color and leave them to the side to dry.

4

To make flags, cut triangles out of colorful paper and tape them to lollipop sticks or wooden toothpicks. When your castle is dry, tape the flags to the top of your towers.

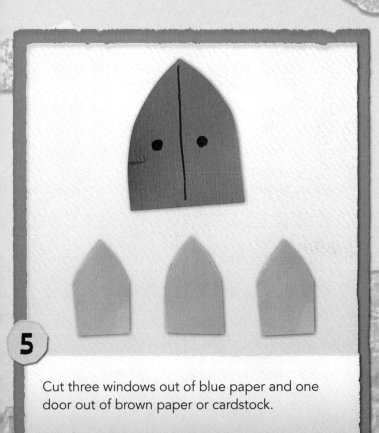

5 Cut three windows out of blue paper and one door out of brown paper or cardstock.

6 Next, tape all three towers together, before sticking on your windows and door.

I AM NOT A TOILET PAPER ROLL...
I'M A HUGE CASTLE!

You don't have to stop at just three toilet paper rolls. Keep taping on more and more painted toilet paper roll towers until you make a super grand castle! You could stick all of your towers onto a painted cardboard box, like this. Have fun designing lots of different door and window shapes as you go.

MERMAID!

PERCHED ON A ROCK NEAR THE SEA SHORE, I SIT AND SING MY MERRY MERMAID SONGS IN THE SUN. WITH MY SHIMMERING TAIL AND LONG HAIR, EVERYONE KNOWS WHO I AM!

TRA, LA, LA, LAAAAAA!

YOU WILL NEED

- ONE EMPTY TOILET PAPER ROLL
- PAINTS & PAINTBRUSHES
- SAFETY SCISSORS
- COLORFUL PAPER
- CARDSTOCK
- GLUE & TAPE
- PEN

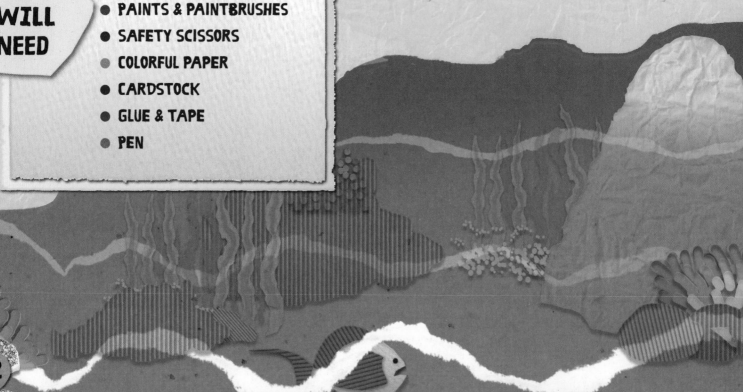

SET THE SCENE

Scrunch up brown paper bags to make a rock for your mermaid to sit on. If you visit the seaside, you could even bring back some pebbles for a rockpool scene. Ready to make your mermaid? Swim over to the next page to find out how.

DID YOU KNOW? A MALE VERSION OF A MERMAID IS CALLED A "MERMAN."

GO FURTHER!

DO YOU WANT TO MAKE SOME COLORFUL CORAL REEFS FOR YOUR MERMAID TO SWIM AROUND AND EXPLORE? WE WILL SHOW YOU HOW ON THE NEXT PAGE.

I'M A MERMAID!

1

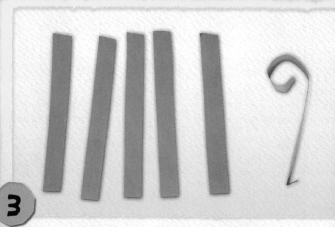

Paint the top half of your toilet paper roll in a flesh color of your choice and the bottom half in a nice, bright color. Leave these to dry.

2

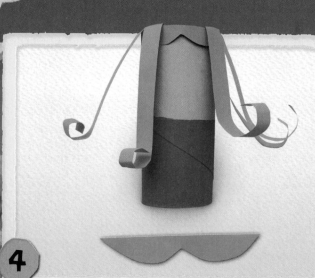

Carefully cut a mermaid tail from some cardstock. Paint this card to match the color of the tail part of your toilet paper roll and leave it to dry.

3

For the hair, cut out strips of colorful paper and roll the ends of each strip around a pencil to make them curl.

4

Now tape each piece of hair to the top of the toilet paper roll. We stuck on some bangs, too!

5

Make a shell bikini from colorful paper and use a black pen to draw on some detail. Now glue the shells in place and draw on a smiley face.

6

Tape the tail to the back of your mermaid and she is ready for any underwater adventure!

I AM NOT A TOILET PAPER ROLL...
I'M A CORAL REEF!

Paint a toilet paper roll turquoise and when it's dry, stick on strips of colorful paper and tissue to look like coral or seaweed. Then, make your own tropical sea creatures and hide them in the bits of coral or seaweed. You can make lots of corals in different colors!

YOUR DESIGNS

NOW IT'S UP TO YOU... THE ONLY THING HOLDING YOUR EMPTY TOILET PAPER ROLLS BACK FROM GREATNESS IS YOUR OWN IMAGINATION! SKETCH YOUR IDEAS HERE—WE'VE GIVEN YOU A COUPLE OF EMPTY ROLLS TO GET YOU STARTED.

. . . .

Shark fins

Shark fins

Bat wings

Googly eyes

Castle door

Unicorn horn

Unicorn ear

Unicorn ear

Mermaid's tail

Pirate hat

Candy cane